Dedicated with love
to my children:

Dorothy… and Rob
Dennis… and Mary
Joanne… and Erik
Beth… and Michael

LISTENING
TO A
TEENAGER

RUTH REARDON

ILLUSTRATED BY
ROLAND RODEGAST

THE C.R. GIBSON COMPANY, NORWALK, CONNECTICUT 06856

Published by The C.R. Gibson Company,
Norwalk, Connecticut 06856
Made in U.S.A.
ISBN 0-8378-8830-1
GB751

I can't jump across the "river"
between childhood
and adulthood.

There is a bridge... of teen years.
It can be lonely, scary, even dangerous...
challenging, exciting and fun.

But it's a one way bridge.
You can help me across.
As I cross, I'll often call for help
(in muffled tones.)
You can help me if you're close,
really close to me,
and if you're really listening!

IT'S WONDERFUL TO BE RESPECTED.
You talk things over with me,
  ask my opinion,
    it's often good advice.
You let me make plans,
  share problems and
    I feel worthwhile,
      contributing to family life.
It's not that great
  when you "let" me share
    in the household jobs!

I'm learning that privileges
  come hand in hand
    with responsibility.
Life is no "free ride."
You're able to watch T.V.
  while I run errands… go off for lunch
    while I baby-sit my brother.
Aren't you glad you have me?
Aren't you glad
  I'm growing up?

ADOLESCENTS CAN BE...
let's see...
What starts with an "A"?
Angry, argumentative, annoying, aggravating.
Why so many negatives?
Let's start again.

Can adolescents be angelic?
No, not really.
How about awesome!
Yes!
That's what we are.
Growing, changing, right before your eyes,
    developing our special personalities,
        leaving behind some childish things
            just like the clothes that we out grew.
Radiating energy,
    bringing hope and newness,
        we're awesome!
If you haven't noticed,
    see beyond the negatives
        to the "awesomeness" of teens!

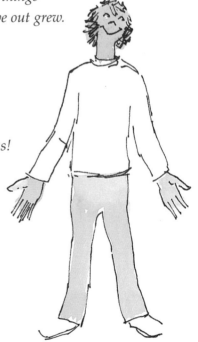

YOU WONDER...
  where is that child
    who adored you?
Who asked questions,
  believing all your answers,
    who said, "please play with me?"
"Let me go with you?"
And talked and talked till you said,
  "Stop".
What happened?

He's here,
  but he has to grow.
He needs space to sort his questions out,
  decide on answers, discover who he is.
He's here.
He's changing
  and that's O.K.
You'll like him.

AS A TODDLER, I OFTEN WENT EXPLORING.
Once I broke dishes in your china cabinet,
pulled up flowers
in the neighbor's garden.
Wandered off
into a stranger's yard.
You said that I was learning
about the world.

I am still exploring...
my curiosity is healthy.
There'll be some broken "dishes,"
yes,
but they can be replaced.
You may think you've lost me in another "yard,"
but I will always come back
if the gate to home
is always open.

IT'S CHALLENGING
 to be a teen today
  and how much more,
   if I am physically
    or mentally challenged.
You may find it even more difficult
 to let me go.
Decide how far,
 then let me go a little further.
Stretch your limits.
Raise your expectations.
I'll have space to be as independent as I can.
Let me try!
Open the world for me...
 higher and wider...
  it's my world too.
I intend to live within it,
 leave my mark - a different one-
  but just as valuable.
That is my challenge.
Let me try to meet it!

SO MANY LEADERS ARE FAILING!
Where are our role models?
Why should I give respect?
It must be earned.

Teach me to value principles
  and to understand
    that they are greater
      than people who betray them.
Show me those who follow them
  so I can decide that I will choose
    to follow them, too!

DO YOU ASSUME THE WORST
  when I go out to parties?
I assume things will be fine.
Are you suspicious?
And think I'm naive?
We're two opposing forces!
If we talk about it...
  really talk, not argue
    maybe we'd find a meeting ground,
      it would not be ideal for either of us,
        but not a battlefield either.
After all, we're on the same side
  aren't we?

I LIKE YOUR SENSE OF HUMOR.
You see the big picture.
I remember how you laughed the time
    when I was little
        and stuck my sandwich
            in the V.C.R. to toast it.
I would be sent to my room
    to think about
        what I had done.
I would hear you laughing
    at my mischief.

Now when I see you
    laughing at yourself
        it takes away some stress
            I put on myself.
I guess we don't have to be perfect...
    always!

By the way, the Principal will call tonight
    to tell you that I skipped class.
I was going for a ride
    but I got caught before
        I left the school yard.
Now is a good time to laugh...
    right?

ONCE A WEEK OR SO
will you take just twenty minutes
to stop and listen?
No interrupting, no comments that are negative:
how can you stand that girl?

That's wrong!
When I was young... what a silly thing to do!

Please listen without censorship.
For I won't be saying only
what I think you want to hear.
I'll talk more,
and you will get to know me better.

How wonderful!
You changed your schedule!
You looked at the hours of each week,
saw where you spent your time and energy
for whom and what
and weighed their importance against
the need I have for you.
Then made space in your schedule for me.
Thanks!
The time will soon be yours again,
but what you give me now
will not be lost.
It will be a part of me... always.

WHEN I WAS VERY LITTLE
  and saw you put your coat on,
    and heard the jingle of your car keys,
      I came running to go with you.
Years passed, and other interests came.
I let you go on errands by yourself!

But now, again,
  you cannot leave the house
    without me.
For I am right beside you!
Isn't that what you have missed?
The weeks I'm learning how to drive
  will end soon...
    getting my license is terrific motivation.
Maybe we can make short trips together
  such fun
    that we will really want to go...
      but I will drive.

JUST SAY "NO"
it sounds so simple,
but when pressure comes
will I just say "YES"?
Fears of being left out, laughed at,
not being accepted,
are strong - maybe strong enough
to make me do what I
really do not want to.

How can I say "NO"?
Only by a strength within, a self-esteem
that comes from knowing I'm worthwhile,
too good to throw away on what destroys.
Your words, and attitude toward me are crucial.

Build me up -
express your love -
make me feel important.
Your opinion helps to lift my head up
so high so I
can look temptation in the eye
and just say "NO"!

"VIRGINITY." THERE, I SAID IT!
It's becoming an unknown word.
Does anybody care
    if it's going out of style?
You talk about safe sex...
        please give equal time to abstinence.

If safe is so important,
    encourage us to be completely safe.
Talk with us about our values,
    morals and higher good.
We'll be safer knowing
    that you care about our future.

As you share yourself with me,
    I'll come to know you,
        not just your role as father.
What you teach
    will take on human form,
        and be integrated in my life.

PLEASE SHARE YOUR FEELINGS
  not just surface talk.
Tell me how you felt
  when you were young,
    and how you feel in life right now.
I can relate to feelings.
They have life and energy.
They are like magnets
  that attract other feelings.
Feelings are the same,
  in any generation.
They are a common ground
  for understanding.

As you open up to me,
  you'll see me opening up to you.
Then we'll not be strangers,
  only sharing common space.

IT ISN'T EASY, BEING IN BETWEEN
childhood and adulthood.
One day I dress my sister's dolls,
    the next I plaster on my makeup
        and walk the mall
            to meet some boys.
You'd have to check my birth certificate
    just to be sure
        what age I am!

Maybe I'm afraid of growing up.
Do you blame me?
I'm taking two steps forward
    then one step back.
But let me set the speed.
I'll get there!

YOU WERE EXCITED, DAD,
  when I told you
    I had joined the school debating team.
Even put your paper down,
  and asked some questions.

It's great you are interested
  in the details of my life–
    my hobbies, classes, likes
      and dislikes.
Knowing me and my interests
  will help in discussing
    the controversial areas
      that lie ahead.

HE'S DEAD!
I can't believe he died!
It was not supposed to be.
So many times he heard,
    "don't drink and drive."
He thought that he could handle it.

Thanks for not lecturing.
We learned the lesson well.
You helped us to express ourselves,
    ask questions, wonder why.
You suggested that we make a memory book
    to give to his parents.

This is our first great loss.
How we handle it
    will be a pattern for our future.

He's dead!
He's actually dead!
He'll never play football again—
    never laugh with us again
        and we will never be the same again.

ARE THERE THINGS YOU WISH YOU HAD,
  or had not done,
    when I was younger?
I wasn't formed in concrete,
  some changes still can be made.
Don't waste time in guilt and regret,
  there can always be new beginnings.

It's never too late ever!
God is timeless.
He can touch our past,
  and shape our future,
    and heal the hurts
      in me...
        and in you!

IF I EVER RETREAT, SORT OF,
into myself,
stay close.
If I only tolerate your hugs,
don't stop.
Keep the arms of your emotions
wrapped securely around me.
Hold me in your love.
Though I turn away,
and hardly talk at all,
always say you love me.
I'll hear your love and store it.
It will not bounce off me.
Your affection will sink into
where I'm hiding.
Soon I'll be full enough
to come out,
and give, in turn,
to you and to others.

EARN MONEY
    save money,
        work.
Money doesn't grow on trees,
    you tell me all the time!

Sure money is important,
    but so are things like having fun,
        acting foolishly,
            taking time to daydream,
                splurging now and then.

Many things
    will help form my character
        and make it rich in ways
            that bank accounts cannot.
Relax a little.
Let's plan to go to Disneyland!
I'll help pay
    by getting another part time job.
Money doesn't grow on trees,
    you know!

WHY DIDN'T I EAT SUPPER,
  or watch T.V.,
    or talk to you?
Because my girlfriend called.
She wants to break up.
I'm devastated!
Probably will never leave my room!
Don't laugh.
Maybe you can call it
  puppy love.
I can't.
To me, it was to be forever.
Even though you say
  there are others-
    understand right now,
      I don't want them.

Take me seriously.
Take some time off
  and spend it with me.
I need you.

"YOU HAVE TO TRY THE BRA ON!"
you scolded in the dressing room
of that small store.
Why couldn't you have whispered?
I heard two women laugh.
I'm so self conscious
-is my body growing right?
Am I the same as others?
Do I really look O.K.?
Is it so terrible to have a drawer full of
fourteen bras that do not fit
because I would not try them on?

Please don't try to choose the clothes I wear.
On shopping trips you say,
"This dress looks wonderful on you."
And coach the sales girl to agree.
If you buy it, it will look wonderful
hanging in my closet.
Or maybe in the drawer,
beside my fourteen bras!

IT'S DIFFERENT NOW
you're trying hard
to fit me in the mold you had
when you were young.
But now the mold is different.
Your world moved more slowly,
and was safer.
Growing up comes faster now
there's more pressure
and more danger.
I have to live in my world,
not in yours.
Some things are still the same though -
they just look different.
We'll discover them together.
They will be the windows
that we need
to see each other's view of life!

PERHAPS YOU SEE ME
  as "another chance."
The things you wanted
  very badly to have,
    or do, or be,
      are transferred, now, to me.
You have my goals,
  my life, my values,
    all planned out,
      wrapped in a package,
        labeled with my name.
But, inside, it's you!

You cannot live your life,
  again, through me.
Love me enough
  to set me free,
    and you can live your own life
      fully and freely.

YOU MIGHT BE SURPRISED!
After being warned by experts
   and other parents,
      to expect the teen turmoil.
Maybe I am one of the few
   who sails right through,
      not causing problems
         (well, not many!)
We're all teenagers
   but each of us is unique!
You don't have to look for trouble
   or worry
      when it doesn't come.
Be thankful.
There's nothing wrong
   if everything
      goes right!

DID YOU KNOW THAT
*   you can really enjoy me?*
Are you letting days and years
*   slip by while worrying*
*   and finding fault?*
Soon I'll be gone.
The telephone will not ring constantly,
*   the radio will not blast loudly,*
*   the house will look*
*   the way you wish.*
There'll be no morning arguments
*   about my clothes.*
Despite the peace, you'll miss me,
*   wonder where the years went.*
Enjoy me now!
I can be a lot of fun.

IT'S HARD TO LET ME GO
but you've been doing it
since you taught me how to walk,
knowing it was the first beginning
of my path away from you.
You have to let me go.
If I feel wrapped
by strings too tight
I'll stumble
and dare not walk on further.

Strings are not just rules,
manipulations,
money,
there are stronger ties
of your emotions.

If you hold me close
to meet your needs,
I'll have to fight to leave.
Or I might decide
the struggle is too hard
and I'll give in.
Then you'll always have me close,
but I will never be
a separate me...
only just a part of you.

I GOT IN TROUBLE
 you're deeply hurt.
You trusted me.
I let you down.
You're disappointed, and afraid,
 blaming yourself, furious at me.
I know that I deserve discipline,
 though I am defiant,
  or sullenly accepting.

Within me is a hurt and frightened child
 who, with support and understanding,
  will get back where I belong.
All has not been lost.
Keep believing in me,
 and in yourselves as parents!

Like the baby you brought home,
 way back,
  I sometimes cry.
I cry alone, and silently,
 not for food, or toys, or my own way,
  I cry for more of you, more understanding.
I hide my tears.
You cannot rush into the nursery to soothe me
 for you will not ever hear me cry
  unless you listen
   for my signals.

WE FILLED FOOD BASKETS
   for Thanksgiving -
      there must have been two hundred!
Well, it sure seemed liked that many!
Our Youth Group never worked so hard -
   especially at home -
      we have a reputation
         to uphold, you know!
We truly care about the homeless,
   victims of war
      and of disasters.
If we seem to be self-centered,
   it's just that growing up
      takes so much time and energy.
When you involve us,
   and we see you helping,
      we don't feel so helpless, quite,
         about the darkness.
We are altruistic, beyond imagination,
   when our energy gets tied to caring
      we'll light not only candles,
         but some real bonfires!
No one
   should ever be hungry.

WHEN I WAS ONLY FOUR
  I was encouraged to make
    a few decisions.
What shirt to wear,
  what socks,
    which friend
      to invite to play.
Big deal! But I was proud.
Now I have to make more
  and more important decisions and
    you may not like what I decide.
When I wore two different colored socks
  to nursery school did it really matter?
So what if people laughed!

When we disagree
  unless it's hurtful, let me decide.
Better that I learn by small mistakes.
Only by making my own decisions
  can I gain the confidence I'll need for
    when I have to make them all by myself.
And, by the way,
  I think
    that now my socks
      will always match!

WHO AM I? WHERE DO I BELONG?
What am I like?
I'm finding out.
That's why
> *I try to be just the same as others*
> *wear the clothes, have the haircut,*
>> *speak the language-*
>>> *be with them all of the time -*
>>> *agree with them and not with you!*
We seem to have some built in magnets,
> *drawing us together.*
It's just another step.
First, close to you,
> *and then a little bit away,*
>> *then joined to them*
>>> *until I find my own identity...*
>>> *in me!*

THE OTHER DAY I SAID,
  "Maybe there is no God!"
No blast of thunder roared.
He doesn't get upset that easily.
These years are times for questioning,
    for confirming
        what till now
            I've just accepted.
My faith will be stronger,
    and more personal
        if I look doubts right in the eye.
You can control some of my actions
    but you can't control what I believe.
Don't worry,
    and don't you provide the thunder.
God has better ways
    to show Himself to me.

I TRIPPED ON THE STAGE
in the school play today!
They laughed!
I wanted to disappear.
It seemed like the end of my world.
I'm never going back to school again!
You sighed,
"that must have been so painful."
And told me of the time
you messed up opening lines.
You understood.
You let me feel really bad,
and hide a while.
I probably will be in class...
tomorrow,
and someday
even laugh about it.
I did look rather funny!
Right now, it hurts too much.
It helps, though,
to see that you agree.

IT CAN'T HAPPEN TO ME!
I'm sure it won't.
I'm young, and I'm strong and -
   agree or not -
      quite smart!
I could fool around
   and not get pregnant
      or catch Aids.
I could experiment
   and not be hooked on drugs.
Swim in the quarries
   and not drown.
Those things happen to others -
   not to me.
You just cannot convince me
   that others
      once believed as I
         and yet it happened,
         yes,
            to them.
So it might also happen,
   yes,
      to me!
Please, help me to realize
   that I am vulnerable,
      and I'd better use my head.

AN "I WON'T" IS OFTEN AN "I CANNOT"
try to see the difference.
Forcing only backfires into more "I won'ts"
if I feel that I cannot.
My pride keeps me from admitting inabilities,
or what I think is inability.
Change your request and avoid the clash.
Look into inabilities
and work with me on confidence.

The behavior that upsets you
is often just a mask to hide my feeling
that I'm not worth much.
I must deny that feeling -
so I can show a picture
of being in control -
of knowing everything.
I have to be the right one, all the time,
for if I'm wrong, I fear exposure.
My best offense is my best defense of course,
so I can blame you and not myself for problems.
Help me to build up my self - esteem,
so I can be... myself.

ISN'T IT O.K. TO ENJOY
  just being on the team?
Do I have to be a star to gain your pride?
Why do we only call grandparents
  after the games we've won?
Are you setting goals for me
  that are so high I'm always stressed?
Will you be pleased with me
  and not always look for medals?
If I do my best in class,
  does it matter what percent I'm in?
Do you love me unconditionally...
  or must I shine, to earn your love?
If I never win a prize,
  will you still be glad I'm yours?

THERE ARE FIVE HUNDRED SNAPSHOTS -
all of me
when I was very little.
You captured the adorable me,
sent pictures off to relatives,
whether they wanted them or not!
How many have you taken of me lately?
Save moments of these teenage years.
It shows me that you value them and me.
I am still important...
with hair too long or strangely styled
or pimples on my face.
Too fat,
too thin,
in clothes you did not choose!
Are you wanting to remember me,
the way I am right now?
How about my room, too?
The very messy one.
You could blackmail me in future years -
when I have teenagers of my own!

I FELT ALMOST GROWN UP LAST NIGHT
  when the two of us went out to dinner.
Like two friends.
I noticed, happily,
   you did not discuss
       the arguments we're having
           about my choice of friends.
You didn't even mention
   the "D" I got in English!
We laughed at family jokes
   solved some of the problems
       in the country,
           and talked about the movies
               that we'd seen,
                   I even left the tip!
I heard you on the phone today
   telling Aunt Susan
       I was getting more mature,
           that you enjoyed the evening
               especially the company!

Cover/book design and production to disk-ready
by Markus Frey, Stamford CT.
Typeset in Palatino italic 11/16 pt.
Printed on Westpoint Offset, 100 lb.